ABOUT THE AUTHORS

Sidney Williams

Sidney Williams is the author of several short stories that have appeared in many anthologies and magazines. He is also a novelist who publishes his work under the pen name of Michael August. Sidney's previous work in comics and graphic novels includes *The Mantus Files*, *The Scary Book*, and *Marauder*. Early in his writing career, Sidney worked as a newspaper reporter covering local news, crime, and entertainment. In addition to writing, Sidney also works in marketing and advertising.

Mark Jones

Born on the outskirts of Manchester in England, Mark has been writing since his early teens. While at college, Mark wrote for the campus magazine and also published poetry in various anthologies. After completing a degree in Communications, Mark worked in a variety of positions, including that of a broadcast assistant at the BBC. Most recently, Mark is employed in Delhi as a writer and editor. He has adapted the classic novel *Kidnapped* into a graphic novel for Campfire.

THE **DUSK** SOCIETY

CAMPFIRE™

THE DUSK SOCIETY

Sitting around the Campfire, telling the story, were:

CHARACTER & STORY CONCEPT **SIDNEY WILLIAMS**

WORDSMITH **MARK JONES**

ILLUSTRATOR **NARESH KUMAR**

COLOURISTS **PRADEEP SINGH SHERAWAT & MANOJ YADAV**

LETTERER **GHANSHYAM JOSHI**

EDITORS **ANDREW DODD & ADITI RAY**

EDITOR (informative content) **RASHMI MENON**

PRODUCTION CONTROLLER **VISHAL SHARMA**

ART DIRECTOR **RAJESH NAGULAKONDA**

COVER ART **NARESH KUMAR & JAYAKRISHNAN K P**

DESIGNER **JAYAKRISHNAN K P**

CAMPFIRE™

www.campfire.co.in

Published by Kalyani Navyug Media Pvt Ltd

101 C, Shiv House, Hari Nagar Ashram

New Delhi 110014

India

www.campfire.co.in

ISBN: 978-81-907829-6-8

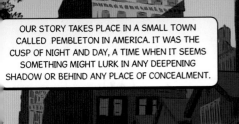

OUR STORY TAKES PLACE IN A SMALL TOWN CALLED PEMBLETON IN AMERICA. IT WAS THE CUSP OF NIGHT AND DAY, A TIME WHEN IT SEEMS SOMETHING MIGHT LURK IN ANY DEEPENING SHADOW OR BEHIND ANY PLACE OF CONCEALMENT.

IF YOU HAVE EVER WALKED HOME ALONE, LATE AT NIGHT, YOU MAY HAVE HAD THE UNEASY FEELING THAT SOMEONE IS WATCHING OR FOLLOWING YOU.

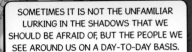

SOMETIMES IT IS NOT THE UNFAMILIAR LURKING IN THE SHADOWS THAT WE SHOULD BE AFRAID OF, BUT THE PEOPLE WE SEE AROUND US ON A DAY-TO-DAY BASIS.

WE TRUST AND COUNT ON SOME OF THEM TO LOVE US AND CARE FOR US. BUT WOULDN'T IT BE DEVASTATING IF WE FOUND OUT WE WERE SIMPLY A PAWN IN THEIR EVIL AND CRUEL LITTLE GAME?

EVERYONE HAS A PAST. THOSE WHOM WE TRUST MAY HAVE THINGS IN THEIR PAST THAT THEY TRY TO HIDE FROM US, EVEN THOUGH IT MAY COST US OUR LIVES.

WHOOSH!

EVEN CLOSE TO HOME, BAD THINGS CAN LURK.

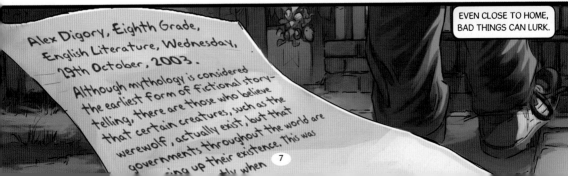

Alex Digory, Eighth Grade, English Literature, Wednesday, 29th October, 2003.

Although mythology is considered the earliest form of fictional story-telling, there are those who believe that certain creatures, such as the werewolf, actually exist, but that governments throughout the world are ...ing up their existence. This was ...tly when

THE GIRL WHOM ISHITA WAS TALKING TO WAS BARBARA LOVE. WITH A BUSY SOCIAL LIFE, BARBARA HAD PAID ISHITA TO GET HER OUT OF SCHOOL FOR THE DAY.

EVERYBODY SHOULD BE CLEARED OUT OF THE BUILDING IN ABOUT FIVE MINUTES, BARBARA.

ISHITA COULD ALWAYS BE COUNTED ON – THAT WAS NEVER AN ISSUE. WHAT WORRIED ME WAS WHETHER SHE COULD BE COUNTED ON TO SAVE THE WORLD OR TO HAPPILY CONTINUE POLLUTING IT.

HOW DID THAT FORMULA GO? WAS THE MIXTURE THREE PARTS OR ONLY TWO? OH WELL, I BETTER THROW IN ALL OF IT JUST TO MAKE SURE.

WHOOSH!

OOPS! IT MUST HAVE BEEN TWO.

LISTEN BARBARA, YOU SHOULD PLAN THIS WEEK OUT, AS WE MIGHT HAVE MORE THAN ONE DAY OFF SCHOOL.

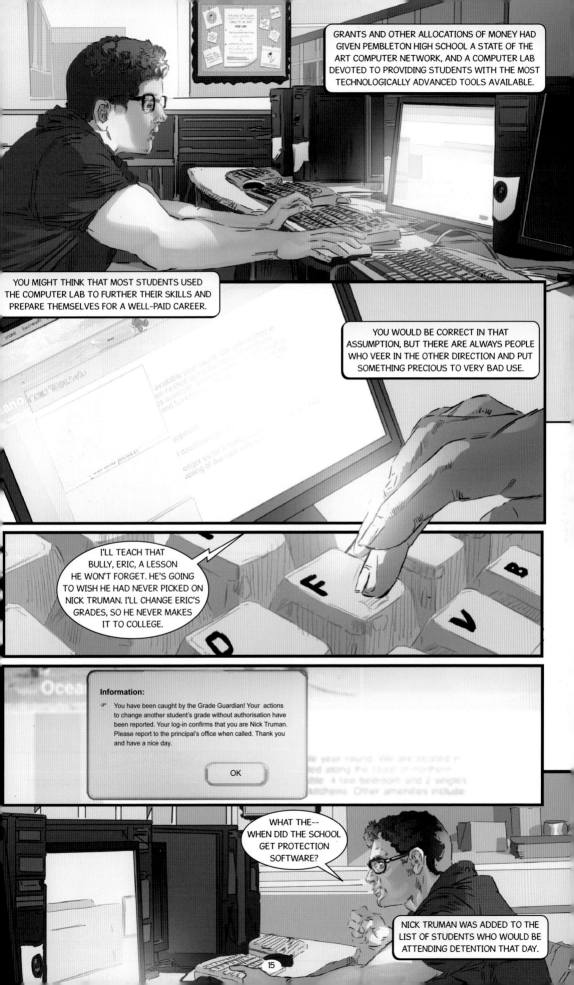

WELCOME TO THE DETENTION CENTRE AT PEMBLETON HIGH SCHOOL, A PLACE WHERE GOOD AFTERNOONS GO TO DIE, WHERE MANY YOUNG PEOPLE DISCOVER THAT IF YOU BREAK THE RULES, YOUR TIME WILL BE STOLEN FROM YOU.

HMM... DETAINED FROM FREEDOM. I ALWAYS WANTED TO KNOW WHAT PRISON FELT LIKE.

ISHITA ALSO FOUND OUT THAT DETENTION AND PRISON HAVE ANOTHER THING IN COMMON – WE GET NO CHOICE AS TO WHO SHARES OUR TIME WITH US.

BE QUIET, ISHITA.

NOW I KNOW – IT CERTAINLY SEEMS TO BE A CHARISMA-FREE ZONE.

YES, DO US ALL A FAVOUR AND SHUT THAT MOUTH OF YOURS – JUST IN CASE YOUR BREATH SMELLS AS BAD AS YOUR CHEMISTRY EXPERIMENTS!

IT WAS NOW OR NEVER. I HAD THEM ALL TOGETHER AT LAST. SOME MYSTERIOUS FORCE HAD BROUGHT MANY SPECIAL CHILDREN TO ONE SCHOOL IN SMALL TOWN AMERICA.

I WAS IN A DILEMMA THAT DAY. I KNEW THAT TWO OF THEM HAD INHERITED SPECIAL POWERS FROM THEIR PARENTS.

HOWEVER, I WAS WORRIED WHETHER ONE OF THEM HAD ALREADY STRUCK A DEAL WITH PIERCEBLOOD.

WELCOME TO THE DETENTION CENTRE. I'D LIKE TO THANK EACH OF YOU FOR JOINING ME THIS AFTERNOON.

I KNOW IT TOOK SOME EFFORT FROM EACH OF YOU. NOW WHO DO WE HAVE WITH US TODAY?

NICK TRUMAN, OR 'MR COMPUTER' AS YOU'RE KNOWN TO YOUR TEACHERS.

ISHITA KUMAR, CHEMISTRY WHIZZ EXTRAORDINAIRE.

AND RONNIE WINSLOW, OR 'SUPER SLACKER' TO YOUR FRIENDS.

BUT SOMEONE IS STILL MISSING.

WHOOSH

OOOPHH! THAT LITTLE TEST SATISFIED MY CURIOSITY. COME ON, LET'S GO HOME.

PIERCEBLOOD WALKED AWAY SATISFIED THAT THE NEW DUSK SOCIETY WAS TO BE A SIGNIFICANT THREAT TO HIM IN THE FUTURE, AND HE WOULD HAVE TO DECIDE WHETHER HE SHOULD DESTROY IT SOONER OR LATER.

VROOMM

THEY'RE LEAVING. PHEW! THAT COULD HAVE BEEN WORSE.

I THINK YOU SHOULD TELL US WHAT'S GOING ON, MISS RAVEN.

THAT WASN'T FUNNY, MISS RAVEN. THAT EXPLOSION COULD HAVE KILLED US ALL, OR GIVEN US THIRD DEGREE BURNS!

I'VE BEEN TRYING, NICK, BUT YOU DON'T SEEM TO BE LISTENING. ALL OF YOU HAVE BEEN CHOSEN TO BECOME MEMBERS OF AN ORGANISATION KNOWN AS THE DUSK SOCIETY.

SO... FROM WHAT I HAVE READ, IT SEEMS THE ANCIENT EGYPTIANS FORESAW THE WORLD WAR. BUT HOW?

'WILLIAM APPROACHED FRIENDS IN THE MILITARY WHO SENT HIM TO A SMALL UNKNOWN OFFICE IN THE HEART OF LONDON, WHERE HIS INTEREST IN EGYPTOLOGY WOULD BE LISTENED TO.'

SO, MR ANDARTON, YOU BELIEVE THAT WITHIN THE ANCIENT REMAINS OF THE EGYPTIANS IS INFORMATION RELATING TO THE FUTURE?

YES, MR KIPLING, I CERTAINLY DO. I WOULD NOT BE WASTING YOUR TIME IF I DID NOT BELIEVE THERE IS SOMETHING IN THIS.

WELL, YOUR MILITARY RECORD IS EXCEPTIONAL, ANDARTON. SO HER MAJESTY'S GOVERNMENT AND I SHOULD, AT THE VERY LEAST, TAKE YOU SERIOUSLY. NOW, HOW CAN MI-6 HELP YOU?

I'LL NEED A GOOD DEAL OF FUNDING, SIR. THERE ARE RUMOURS ABOUT A MAN CALLED HOWARD CARTER. IT SEEMS HE MAY HAVE FOUND SOMETHING IN EGYPT. SOMETHING VERY IMPORTANT.

14th March 1923

Full Subject Name: Doctor Adam Rillion Pierceblood
Age: Unknown
Nationality: Suspected Romanian national
Height: 5 feet 11 inches
Hair: Blonde
Eyes: Green

Section Report: As of today, I have a good man called William Andarton compiling a full report on Pierceblood. However, due to the urgent nature of your request, I have noted below what little information we have on the subject.

All the evidence I am presenting you with should be handled with care; it is very difficult to find concrete information on Pierceblood. MI-6 spent a lot of money bribing criminal suspects such as forgers, gun runners, thieves, and fences. Unfortunately, a great deal of misinformation was fed back to us, which is very embarrassing indeed.

So far, we suspect that Pierceblood is an expert on the occult and is well connected, with links to some fanatical occult elements.

Rumour has it that Pierceblood lost a great deal of his occult artefact collection when the Titanic sunk in 1912. The artefacts were seemingly smuggled aboard the doomed ocean liner in cars and some passenger luggage. That would lead us to believe that Pierceblood may have a base of operation in New York. It seems his renewed collection of artefacts coincided with the World War.

German intelligence officers informed us that their efforts to locate religious artefacts during the war were hampered by another party. They would not confirm that party to be Pierceblood, but reported that they had been alerted to the presence of a man who seemed to be well funded and known in occult circles.

Our latest operative, William Andarton, claims to have recently encountered Pierceblood in the tomb of none other than Tutankhamun. An artefact known as the Weres amulet was taken from the tomb by Pierceblood, who stated that it had the power to bring the dead back to life. With the body of Tutankhamun missing, we cannot take any chances, so I have suggested that Andarton should try to collect as many artefacts as he can before Pierceblood does.

As William Andarton will probably get killed on this, as I consider it, suicide mission, I recommend that we have him knighted. If he is killed, government support would be fully behind us, following the death of a Knight of the Realm.

Yours faithfully,

SR Kipling
Acting head of MI-6

WHEN IT IS OPENED, I WILL REMAKE THE WORLD IN MY IMAGE, AND THEN I WILL COME AFTER YOU AND THE SCUM THAT YOU REPRESENT. SO WHY DON'T YOU GIVE UP NOW WHILE YOU CAN!

ENOUGH TALK, PIERCEBLOOD LET THEM HAVE IT, ARJUNA!

TWANG

SWHOOSH

'OCCASIONALLY, SIR WILLIAM FOUND A WAY TO DEFEAT ONE OF PIERCEBLOOD'S HENCHMEN. AN ARROW, SMEARED WITH THE BLOOD OF A HYDRA AND THEN LIT, ELIMINATED A REANIMATED MUMMY, ONE OF PIERCEBLOOD'S NEW HENCHMEN.'

AARGHHHH!

IT BURNS!

'AFTER HIS ENCOUNTER WITH PIERCEBLOOD'S NEW FRIENDS, SIR WILLIAM REALISED HE WOULD NOT ONLY BE BATTLING MAGIC, BUT ALSO SCIENCE – THE DARK SIDE OF SCIENCE.'

NICE WORK, ARJUNA. IT'S TIME WE RECRUITED MORE GOOD MEN LIKE YOU.

'SIR WILLIAM FINALLY REALISED THAT HE COULD NOT OPPOSE PIERCEBLOOD ON HIS OWN.'

'SO, IN 1941, HE ASSEMBLED A GROUP OF EXPERTS, WHO WERE DEVOTED TO THE PUREST OF MAGIC. THERE WERE WIZARDS, SOMETIMES CALLED MAGES, AND OTHER MEN OF SCIENCE AND GREAT INTELLECT. HE NAMED THE GATHERING THE DUSK SOCIETY.'

THIS ORGANISATION WILL BE KEPT HIDDEN FROM THE REST OF THE WORLD, MR PRESIDENT. I HAVE WORD FROM SIR WILLIAM HERE THAT THE DUSK SOCIETY WILL UTILISE THE BEST OF OUR SOCIETIES, WHILST PRESERVING THE LIVES OF THE MAJORITY.

THAT'S GOOD TO HEAR, PRIME MINISTER. THE AMERICAN PUBLIC, WHOM I REPRESENT, WILL NEVER KNOW OF THIS MEETING OR THE POWERS INVESTED IN THOSE WHO HAVE ATTENDED IT.

YES, SECRECY HAS TO BE MAINTAINED AT ALL COSTS.

ALL OF YOU WILL USE YOUR WILES AND YOUR TALENTS TO HELP US FIND MEMBERS OF PIERCEBLOOD'S CULT IN PEMBLETON.

WE'VE SEEN THAT ALL OF YOU ARE GOOD AT IMPROVISING. I WILL HELP YOU AS MUCH AS I CAN, BUT CONSIDER THIS MISSION YOUR INITIATION CEREMONY.

I THINK YOU NEED TO START WORKING AS A TEAM, AND DECIDE WHAT YOUR NEXT MOVE WILL BE. SO GOODBYE FOR NOW, AND BE CAREFUL OUT THERE.

OKAY, HOW AND WHERE DO WE START? HOW DO WE TRACK DOWN THIS PIERCEBLOOD CHARACTER?

HE'S PROBABLY KEEPING A LOW PROFILE IN PEMBLETON, HIDING OUT IN AN EMPTY PROPERTY.

WE DON'T HAVE TIME TO CHECK EVERY VACANT HOUSE IN PEMBLETON, ISHITA.

YOU'RE A COMPUTER EXPERT, NICK.

I'M SURE YOU CAN GET YOUR COMPUTER TO SAVE US SOME TIME.

YOU REALLY THINK WE CAN FIND PIERCEBLOOD?

NICK, PIERCEBLOOD WILL FIND US FIRST. THEN WHEN WE'RE ASLEEP IN BED, HE'LL--

SHUT UP, RONNIE!

LISTEN, MY FATHER'S A REPORTER. HE'S ALWAYS TALKING ABOUT PAPER TRAILS. MAYBE WE CAN USE HIS SUGGESTIONS TO FIGURE OUT WHERE PIERCEBLOOD'S FAN CLUB IS MEETING UP. I'LL CALL HIM NOW.

SOUNDS LIKE A PLAN. WHEN YOU'RE DONE, I'LL DRIVE US ALL TO MY PLACE.

QUICK, BEFORE THEY EAT US FOR DINNER!

THOSE DOGS RUSHED AT THE MEMBERS AS IF SATAN HIMSELF HAD GIVEN THEM ORDERS. BUT THE ORDERS HAD COME FROM SOMEONE MUCH WORSE... PIERCEBLOOD.

GGRRRRF

GRROWWL!

START THE CAR, NICK! PLEASE GET US OUT OF HERE NOW!

GGRRRRF

I'M TRYING, BUT THE ACCELERATOR--

THAT'S IT! IT'S WORKING.

VROOMM

WELL ISHITA, THAT DEFINITELY SEEMS TO BE A SITE SOMEONE DOESN'T WANT INVESTIGATED.

CHECKING THE LAND TITLE OFFICE TOMORROW MORNING SOUNDS LIKE A GOOD IDEA. SEE IF YOU CAN FIND OUT WHO OWNS THAT PROPERTY. NOW ALL OF YOU GO HOME AND GET SOME SLEEP.

WHAT DID YOU FIND OUT, NICK?

NOTHING, ISHITA. SOMEONE HAD TORN THE OWNERSHIP DETAILS FROM THE PROPERTY FILE.

SO, YOU ARE CONVINCED THAT SOMEONE TAMPERED WITH THE PUBLIC RECORDS DATABASE, NICK?

ABSOLUTELY, MISS RAVEN. I EVEN CALLED THE ADMINISTRATOR. HE TOLD ME HE THINKS A HACKER BROKE INTO THE DATABASE, AND DELETED THE ADDRESS DETAILS.

WELL. FROM WHAT YOU HAVE TOLD ME... HERE'S MY TAKE ON WHAT MIGHT HAVE HAPPENED AT THAT HOUSE.

I TOLD YOU BEFORE ABOUT PIERCEBLOOD TRYING TO UNLOCK A DOORWAY BETWEEN WORLDS. PERHAPS HE'S TRYING TO DO IT AGAIN, BUT THE CEREMONY WENT WRONG. THAT WOULD EXPLAIN THE FIRE DAMAGE TO THE PROPERTY.

SO, A BURNT OUT HOUSE AND SOME SYMBOLS – NOT MANY CLUES TO FOLLOW. THIS REMINDS ME OF MY TIME IN PARIS AS A NEW RECRUIT OF THE DUSK SOCIETY.

THAT WAS NEARLY THIRTY YEARS AGO...

WHAT CAN YOU TELL ME, INSPECTOR DELON?

WHY WOULD SHE HAVE MAKE-UP ON HER NECK?

SAME AS THE OTHER MURDERS – THE BODY HAS BEEN DRAINED OF BLOOD AND HAS BITE MARKS. THERE IS BLACK AND WHITE MAKE-UP SMEARED ON ONE SIDE OF HER NECK TOO.

MADEMOISELLE, I HAVE NO IDEA. BUT I DO NOT BELIEVE IT WAS HER MAKE-UP. ONE THING I HAVE NOTICED IS THAT THE MURDERER ALWAYS KILLS AT NIGHT.

'IN 1974, PARIS WAS THE SCENE OF A SLEW OF MURDERS. ALL THE VICTIMS HAD SIMILAR BITE MARKS ON THEIR BODIES, AND ALL SEEMED TO HAVE BEEN KILLED AT NIGHT. FRUSTRATED BY THE LACK OF PROGRESS IN THE INVESTIGATION, THE FRENCH PRESIDENT HAD ASKED THE DUSK SOCIETY FOR HELP.'

'THERE WERE FEW CLUES TO THE CASE. I SUSPECTED THE INVOLVEMENT OF A VAMPIRE DUE TO THE LACK OF BLOOD IN THE BODIES OF THE VICTIMS. BUT MAKE-UP?'

TWO HOURS LATER.

TAP TAP TAP

TENACITY IS THE TOOL OF THE SUCCESSFUL. THE PEOPLE WHO USE IT BEST ARE THOSE WHO DON'T GIVE UP, AND DON'T LET PROBLEMS PERSIST WHEN THEY KNOW THEY CAN BE SOLVED.

ISHITA KUMAR WAS NEVER ONE TO LET AN AUTHORITY FIGURE, LIKE DARIELLE'S DAD, GET IN HER WAY.

TAP TAP TAP

WHO'S THERE? BILLY THORNCRUP, IF THAT IS YOU AGAIN, I WILL CALL THE POLICE, I SWEAR!

TELL YOUR DAD TO GET A NEW TREE. THIS ONE IS TERRIBLE TO CLIMB. SO, ARE YOU GOING TO OPEN THE WINDOW OR NOT?

SORRY ABOUT WHAT HAPPENED WITH MY DAD BEFORE. HE'S UPSET... IT'S JUST THAT HE'S...

OVER FORTY? YEAH, THAT MUST BE DISTRESSING FOR HIM. NOW, I DON'T SUPPOSE YOU HAVE A SAMPLE OF THE DUST THAT WAS LEFT BEHIND WHEN YOUR BROTHER VANISHED?

ISHITA COLLECTED THE SAMPLE FROM DARIELLE AND WENT STRAIGHT HOME. IN HER FATHER'S GARAGE, SHE USED HER OWN EQUIPMENT TO ANALYSE IT.

ALRIGHT RONNIE, MY BLUETOOTH IS ON, SO YOU SHOULD BE HEARING ME LOUD AND CLEAR. WHY DON'T YOU SA SOMETHING JUST SO I KNOW YOU'RE THERE?

60

THE ASWANG, ONE OF PIERCEBLOOD'S MOST DREADED OPERATIVES, HAD KEPT AN INVISIBLE PRESENCE DURING THE FIRST ATTACK ON THE DUSK SOCIETY AT THEIR HIGH SCHOOL. BUT HE NOW CROUCHED IN THE DARKNESS, WAITING TO TARGET THE NEW MEMBERS.

WAS HE UNDER THE ORDERS OF PIERCEBLOOD AND HIS GANG? THE DUSK SOCIETY WERE ABOUT TO FIND OUT.

The address seems correct, but where are those kids?

IF THEY HAVE ALREADY LEFT, THEN IT'S TIME WE WERE INTRODUCED. I THINK I'LL HAVE THE FIRST DANCE!

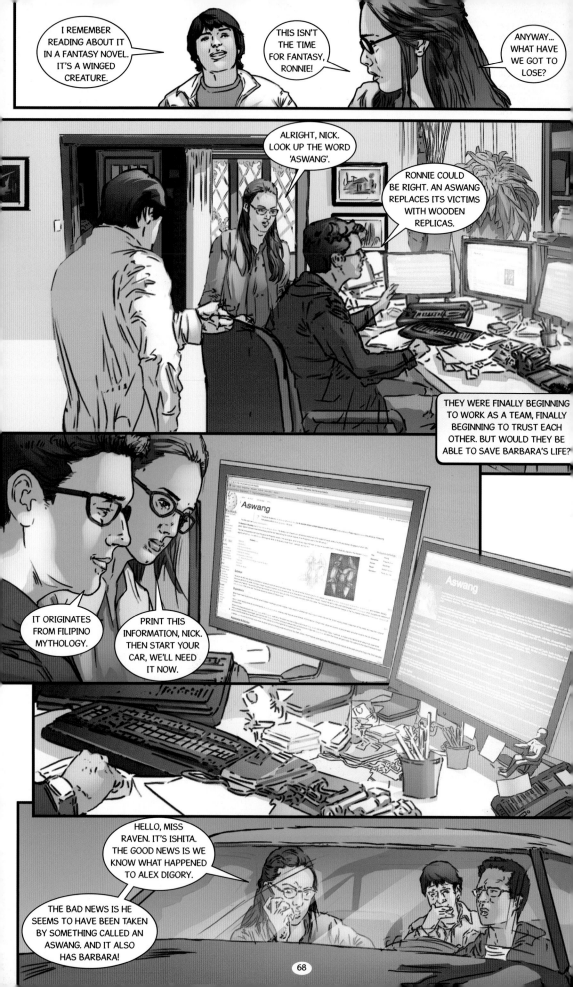

SO WHAT WAS PIERCEBLOOD PLANNING?

THAT PIERCEBLOOD... HE WANTS TO CREATE A UTOPIA. THE ASWANGS WILL HELP HIM DESTROY WHOLE SOCIETIES, SO HE CAN REBUILD THE WORLD AS HE SEES FIT.

PIERCEBLOOD ALSO WANTED MY KIDS FOR SOMETHING.

BUT, IF YOU GO AFTER THE ASWANGS, YOU NEED TO KNOW THEIR HISTORY.

HAVE YOU EVER HEARD ABOUT THE THEORY THAT PTERODACTYLS WERE NOT FROM PLANET EARTH? WELL, IT'S TRUE.

'AND THE ASWANGS, THE ONES WE KNOW TODAY, ARE DESCENDED FROM THE PTERODACTYLS WHO LIVED IN THIS WORLD IN PREHISTORIC TIMES.'

'THEY COME FROM ANOTHER DIMENSION. BUT THEY ADAPTED AND STAYED AFTER THE PTERODACTYLS DIED OUT. THEIR VICIOUS TEMPERS MEANT THEY WOULD DO ANYTHING TO SURVIVE.'

'THEIR SHAPE-SHIFTING ABILITIES ALLOWED THEM TO SURVIVE AMONGST MEN.'

'THE ASWANGS ARE MUCH MORE POWERFUL THAN THE PTERODACTYLS EVER WERE. THEIR ABILITIES ARE INCREDIBLE. BUT THERE AREN'T MANY OF THEM IN OUR WORLD, MAYBE TWO OR THREE AT THE MOMENT.'

'BUT THEIR ANCESTORS MAY BE EVEN MORE POWERFUL BY NOW. IF PIERCEBLOOD CAN SUMMON ENOUGH POWER TO OPEN THEIR DIMENSIONAL DOORWAY, THE WORLD COULD BE FLOODED WITH FAR MORE DEVELOPED AND POWERFUL ASWANGS.'

'SOMETHING... SOME UNKNOWN MAGIC... CLOSED THAT DOORWAY EONS AGO. BUT THOSE WHO FOLLOW PIERCEBLOOD HAVE BEEN TRYING TO OPEN THAT DOORWAY. THEY HAVE BEEN WORKING WITH AN ASWANG – THE WAY THEIR GROUP HAS ALWAYS WORKED WITH SUPERNATURAL BEINGS.'

'IF THEY CAN OPEN THE DIMENSIONAL DOORWAY, THEY WILL RELEASE AN ENTIRE SOCIETY OF ASWANGS ON EARTH. THE ASWANGS WOULD THEN GO TO WAR WITH EVERY POWER, DESTROYING ANYTHING THAT GETS IN THEIR WAY. THEY CONSIDER THIS TO BE A 'CLEANSING' OF THE WORLD. THEN PIERCEBLOOD CAN INITIATE A REBOOT AND RESHAPE THE WORLD TO HIS WILL.'

AND THAT WOULD EXPLAIN WHY PIERCEBLOOD DIDN'T KILL US AT THE SCHOOL THAT FIRST TIME. ONE OF US COULD BE A WHITE MAGE – THE VERY CHESS PIECE HE NEEDS TO WIN THE GAME.

NOW I KNOW EVERYTHING. I BETTER TELL... WAIT, IF DOCTOR CRIGLER IS THE ASWANG, THEN RONNIE AND NICK... I'VE GOT TO WARN THEM!

WHILE ISHITA HAD BEEN SPEAKING WITH MR DIGORY, NICK AND RONNIE HAD BEEN TRYING TO GAIN ACCESS TO DOCTOR CRIGLER'S HOUSE.

LOOKS LIKE A REGULAR HOUSE. YOU KNOW I WAS EXPECTING--

A HAUNTED MANSION, LIKE SOMETHING OUT OF *RESIDENT EVIL*?

YEAH, EXACTLY.

YOU KNOW, I DON'T FEEL MAGICALLY POWERFUL. DO YOU? I THINK WE'RE ON OUR OWN. MAYBE WE'RE JUST REGULAR GUYS, AND ISHITA AND BARBARA HAVE ALL THE POWERS.

BUZZZZZ

THAT WOULD BE JUST OUR LUCK, RONNIE.

THE FORCES OF DARKNESS DON'T SEEM TO BE AT HOME. DO WE GO IN OR NOT?

79

CRACK! CRACK! CRACK!

BUT NEITHER PIERCEBLOOD NOR HIS FRIENDS WERE GOING TO WAIT AROUND FOR RONNIE TO ATTACK THEM.

I'LL MAKE THE DUSK SOCIETY PAY FOR THIS! DO YOU MEDDLING KIDS HEAR ME? I SAID I'LL MAKE YOU PAY!

WE'LL REGROUP LATER. FOR NOW... RUN!

I'LL GET RONNIE.

OKAY, I'LL CHECK ON BARBARA AND ALEX.

WHAT HAPPENED?

I THINK WE WITNESSED THE BIRTH OF A WHITE MAGE. OH, AND YOU SAVED THE WORLD BY CLOSING THE ASWANG ANCESTORS OFF IN THE OUTER DARKNESS.

COOL, SO ARE YOU GOING TO GO OUT WITH ME THEN? I WAS SERIOUS WHEN I SAID YOU HAD NICE EYES.

RELAX RONNIE, YOU'RE IN SHOCK. IT'S GIVING YOU DELUSIONS.

WHAT ABOUT YOU BARBARA, ARE YOU OKAY?

I'M FINE.

YOU MUST BE ALEX.

YES.

83

BY THE TIME I ARRIVED AT DOCTOR CRIGLER'S HOUSE, THE NEW DUSK SOCIETY HAD ALREADY DEFEATED PIERCEBLOOD. THE RESULTING EXPLOSIONS, STRANGE LIGHTS, AND A RAMPAGING ASWANG MEANT THAT HALF THE NEIGHBOURHOOD HAD CALLED THE POLICE.

THE OTHER HALF OF THE NEIGHBOURHOOD WERE MORE INTELLIGENT, AND HAD HID THEMSELVES IN THEIR BASEMENTS.

I THOUGHT I TOLD YOU TO WAIT, ISHITA!

ARE YOU JOKING, MISS RAVEN? THE WORLD WOULD HAVE BEEN OVERRUN WITH ASWANGS IF WE HAD.

ISHITA TOLD ME EVERYTHING THAT HAD HAPPENED. SHE HAD BEEN SURPRISED TO FIND OUT WHO THE WHITE MAGE WAS. IT SEEMS SHE HAD PLACED LITTLE FAITH IN RONNIE WINSLOW WHEN THEY FIRST MET.

YOU HAVE ALL PROVED YOURSELVES WORTHY TO BE MEMBERS OF THE DUSK SOCIETY. BUT I MUSTN'T FORGET...

...MR XIAO, CAN YOUR TEAM TRACK DOWN THE ASWANG?

YES, THEN WE WILL BRING PIERCEBLOOD TO JUSTICE.

PIERCEBLOOD... WHEN HE ATTACKED THE SCHOOL WITH THAT EXPLOSION, MISS RAVEN MADE RONNIE AND BARBARA STAND NEXT TO HER--

BECAUSE THEY HAVE MAGIC POWERS, AND WE DON'T.

ON THE CONTRARY, NICK. YOU WORKED YOUR SHARE OF MAGIC, BUT OF A SCIENTIFIC KIND. YOU WITH YOUR COMPUTER. ISHITA WITH HER CHEMISTRY. JUST LIKE THE DUSK SOCIETY OF OLD: A COMBINATION OF MAGIC AND SCIENCE.

I HAVE AN EYE FOR TALENT, AND I'M SURE ALL OF YOUR ABILITIES WILL BE PUT TO GOOD USE AGAIN SOMETIME IN THE NEAR FUTURE. NOW, ENJOY THE REST OF YOUR NIGHT. AFTER ALL, IT IS HALLOWEEN!

HISTORY'S BELIEVE IT OR NOT!

WHAT IS A CURSE?

A curse is the opposite of a blessing. It causes bad luck to a person or thing. Curses create misfortunes such as sickness, accidents, or in some cases, even death.

It is claimed that the effectiveness of a curse can vary. A curse may last for a few days, but in other cases, it can remain for thousands of years. An example of the latter is the curse of Tutankhamun. Let's learn more about this legendary curse.

WHO WAS TUTANKHAMUN?

He was an Egyptian pharaoh. He was nine years old when he became a pharaoh, and ruled for nearly ten years! He is also popularly known as 'Tutankhamun: the boy king'.

THE CURSE OF TUTANKHAMUN

Led by an Englishman named Howard Carter, a team of archaeologists discovered the tomb of Tutankhamun in 1922, and unravelled its treasures the following year. The mummy inside the tomb was in perfect condition. It was one of the most sensational discoveries in history. However, one thing that the archaeologists chose to ignore was the warning written in ancient hieroglyphics at the entrance to the tomb:

'Death will come to those who disturb the sleep of the Pharaoh'

It is thought that the warning was a curse. It is widely believed that the Curse of Tutankhamen has caused misfortune, and sometimes even death. The affected includes men who were part of the excavation team back in 1922.

The curse seems to have resurfaced in recent times. In 1992, a popular news channel sent a team of filmmakers to make a documentary about the Curse of Tutankhamun. Several of the filmmakers suffered accidents while working on the documentary.

Does the Curse of Tutankhamun really exist? It could be nothing more than a series of coincidences. Believe it or not!

MYTHS AND MONSTERS FROM AROUND THE WORLD

Unexplained incidents create breeding ground for myths and monsters. Enter 'Myth Mansion' to find out more about mysterious and mythical creatures.

Dracula

Dracula is a villain in Bram Stoker's classic novel, *Dracula*, and his character was inspired by a Romanian prince called Vlad III Dracula. In Romanian, 'drac' means devil. The prince was famous for being both oppressive and cruel. According to most versions of this legend, vampires are attractive and forever young. They also have supernatural strength. Vampires can transform themselves into animals like bats or wolves. They bite their victims and drink their blood. Romanian legends gave rise to the belief that if you get bitten by a vampire, you too will become a vampire after you die.

Aswang

A popular monster in Filipino myths and legends, this beast is also called *tik-tik* because of the sound it makes. It is said that if an Aswang is near a victim, the sound – heard by the victim – appears to come from far away.

That is how they are said to trick people. The Aswang usually appears as a shy person during the day, and a monster during the night. Besides contributing to entertaining stories, mothers use the Aswang myth to stop their children from staying out at night and causing mischief!

The Aswang has become so famous that every year, in Roxas City, Philippines, an Aswang festival takes place. It's just like Halloween!

Frankenstein's Creature

In Mary Shelley's novel, *Frankenstein*, a hideous creature is created by a scientist named Victor Frankenstein. In his attempt to create life using inanimate matter, Victor meddles with nature, and ends up assembling a creature that he cannot control. Eventually, the creature attacks his creator, and is seen as a monster. Frankenstein's creature is seen as an example of science going out of control. The character is now one of the most famous monsters in the history of literature and films.

SOME PEOPLE SAY THAT THESE MONSTERS ACTUALLY EXIST, AND SOME SAY THAT THEY DON'T. IT'S UP TO YOU TO BELIEVE IT OR NOT!